Fourteen years after retirement and still not retired!

Published in the United States by House of Walker Publishing , LLC (HWP) Elizabeth, New Jersey 07208

All rights Reserved. No part of this publication may be reproduced or transmitted in any form or by any means, electronic or mechanical, including photocopying, recording, or any other information storage or retrieval system, without the written permission from the publisher, House of Walker Publishing, LLC

Permissions: Manuscript presented by: Clinton Miller Jr. with all applicable permissions

Cover art by: Clinton Miller Jr.
Library of Congress Control Number: 2022902748
Copyright © 2018 by Clinton Miller Jr.
ISBN: 978-1-957775-01-2

**Recipes were given by friends and family of Clinton Miller Jr. Permissions to use acquired. Neither he, nor anyone associated with the compilation of recipes in this book, are responsible for any adverse reactions one may incur from the use of any of the ingredients.

Table of Contents

Dedication……………………………………………........i
Testimonials………………………………………………ii
About ELIC (English language Institute/China)………........iii

The Food

Appetizers & Beverages………………………………..1
Bread & Muffins…………………………………….......9
Soups, Stews, Salads & Sauces………………………....17
Beef, Pork & Lamb……………………………….........29
Seafood, Poultry, Pasta & Casseroles………………........37
Deserts, Pies, Cakes & Cookies………………………....47
Forever love………………………………………….....61
Miscellaneous……………………………………….....71
Vegetables & Side Dishes……………………………....75
A Word………..79
About the author…………………………………..........81

INDEX

Cooking terms………………………………….....…….. 85
Measurement abbreviations……………………………....87
Conversions…………………………………………......88
Index of recipes……………………………….....……….89
Index of contributors…………………………….............92
Notes………………………………………………….....95

Dedication

To my beloved wife Jacquelyn, family & friends

First, I would like to thank my God for planting the vision of this trip to China in my heart. Secondly, I appreciate and thank those who have prayed for me, encouraged me, and sowed into my life and into this cookbook venture. A portion of the proceeds from the sale of this cookbook helped to fund my 2014 trip to Asia with the English Language Institute/China (ELIC). Words cannot express my gratitude. I will never forget your kindness and I'll be taking you with me in my heart.

This cookbook is dedicated to my late wife, Jacquelyn, who was a fantastic cook and baker. She loved to cook, and I love to eat! Jacque was also a lady of great creative gifts with a loving and giving heart. God blessed us to find each other and throughout our marriage, He continued to bless us exceedingly and abundantly above all we could have asked or thought.

Jacquelyn received her Masters Degree in School Counseling on May 15, 2001, which was 10 years after we were married. Our wedding took place on May 18, 1991, a day that I will always remember. Had Jacquelyn lived, May 18, 2021, we would have celebrated our 30th anniversary.

You will find this book to be quite different from any other cookbook in that you will have an opportunity to experience personal and intimate photos of Jacquelyn and myself. You will also read reflections from friends and family members as they share their thoughts about us.

It is my prayer that you prosper and be in good health even as your soul prospers. May you have good success in whatever you put your hands, heart, and minds to do. May the Lord bless you and keep you as His goodness and mercy follow you all the days of your life.

Remember, I love you and there's absolutely nothing you can do about it!

This is only the beginning; for the best is yet to come for you and for me.

Shalom,
Bro. Clinton Miller, Jr.

Testimonials

Majid Tehranian (1937-2012) said, "In dialogue, we change through mutual appreciation, sympathy, and empathy. This is not the easiest method of human communication, but it is the most fruitful."

"Cook `N with Clinton," shares not only International and Indigenous recipes, it also shares cooking terms with an accurate index.

Evacuate and read, "Cook `N with Clinton," after this Global Covid Pandemic. Please share this fruit of Miller's labor with friends and family. Finally, from the cover page to the end you will be greeted with unconditional love.

Mary Dozier-Mendez
President and CEO, Wisdom Educational Group

"My brother loves to eat and will even trade flowers for a great meal. I'm proud that he has all his eating delights under one cover. He will cook under duress, and he has eaten many of these dishes. I do enjoy when we cook together via zoom."

Wendy

As Clinton's siblings, we are very excited about his venture to Asia and the work that he will be doing and the students that he will be teaching. We are praying for your safe travels there and back home. We love you, Bro!

Clint

English language Institute – China

Since 1981, ELIC has been placing passionately committed people in teaching roles across Asia, who primarily serve through the medium of English instruction. They accomplish this through recruiting, training, and sending men and women from the USA, Canada, and other countries, to meet the ever-growing demand for quality English education in Asia. The comprehensive graduate-level training provided to their new teachers has raised the bar significantly in the countries where they serve. Ongoing professional development opportunities for their teachers include earning Master's degrees, graduate certificate programs, and two Ph.D. options.

They have vibrant programs for college students, graduates, singles, couples, families, and second-career adults. The present countries of service include China, Mongolia, Laos, Vietnam, Cambodia, and Myanmar. In most cases, they maintain both year-long and summer programs. While focused primarily on university campuses and teacher training, they teach in a variety of other settings designed to best serve the host countries and government entities. They are committed to working with the host countries and government agencies to design teaching programs to best meet their ever-changing needs. Increasingly this includes supplying key industry experts from the West to engage with their Asian counterparts through lectures and roundtable discussions. In the coming year, ELIC is excited to be adding new teaching programs in both Mongolia and Laos. In China, Spanish language teachers are now being sent to complement the English language teams on university campuses.

teach@elic.org p. 800.366.3542
Available M-Th, 7am-6pm MDT

Cook'n with Clinton

Appetizers & Beverages

PINEAPPLE-CARROT JUICE
H. Jerome Youman III

2 c. pineapple juice
2 diced carrots
1¼ in. thick, peeled lemon slice
¼ c. ice

Process all ingredients in a blender until juice is smooth and ice is melted. Makes 3 cups.

OLD-FASHIONED LEMONADE
Drew Miller

5 to 6 lemons
1 c. sugar
2 qt. cold water

Slice the lemons in ½ and squeeze each of them into a large measuring cup. This should yield about 1 ½ cups of juice. Remove any seeds. In a large pitcher, combine the juice and sugar. Stir in the cold water and serve over ice. Tip: For an interesting touch, place mint leaves in the ice cube trays before freezing. Makes about 10 cups.

BRUSCHETTA
Ray Halpin

3 ripe medium tomatoes, diced
¼ lb. of Smoked Salmon, diced
6 oz. Mozzarella cheese, diced strips (chiffonade)
½ Medium onion diced
12 Kalamata olives diced
1 T. Fresh Basil cut in thin

Place all ingredients in a bowl. Dress with extra virgin olive oil, salt and pepper, mix. Let rest for an hour or so. Serve with good bread, toasted and rubbed with garlic. You can add more of less of any ingredient depending upon what you like. Bruschetta is, after all, at its simplest, toast with garlic and olive oil.

Every five years after our wedding, we celebrated by renewing our vows. This is one of those celebrations

Appetizers & Beverages

SWEET N SOUR MEATBALLS

Mary Green

1 bag of frozen meatballs, beef or turkey (1 oz. size)

Sauce:
4 cups water   ½ cup cornstarch
2 cups cider vinegar   ½ cup soy sauce
2 cups ketchup

Unthaw meatballs and bake @ 350 for 30-45 minutes. For sauce, mix together and heat the above ingredients in a saucepan. Allow sauce to thicken. Continue to heat until the sauce just starts to bubble. Pour sauce over meatballs.

This recipe will make a hit for any occasion. You will be asked to make it all the time.

ITALIAN PARTY BITES

From Jacque's Recipe Box

1 loaf Italian bread shell (12 inches)   1 tsp. onion, minced
1 tsp. Italian seasoning   ½ tsp. thyme leaves
½ cup mozzarella cheese, shredded   1 tbsp. olive oil
1 cup thinly sliced vegetables (bell peppers, onions, etc.)
1 can (2.2 oz.) black olives, sliced and drained
¼ cup Parmesan cheese, shredded

Preheat oven to 450° F. Place bread shell on a cookie sheet. In a bowl, toss together minced onion, Italian seasoning, mozzarella cheese, thyme leaves, olive oil and vegetables; spread mixture over bread shell. Top with olives and Parmesan cheese. Bake for 8-10 minutes. Cut into 2-inch squares.

Appetizers & Beverages

PARTY MEATBALLS (Ann and Fran Brantley)

Francena Brantley

2 lbs. pork sausage
1 lb. ground beef
2 eggs
1 cup cornflakes crushed
Garlic salt or powder, to taste

Salt and pepper to taste
6 small onions chopped
1 cup regular mustard
1 cup vinegar
1 cup sugar

Mix first 6 ingredients well. Form into small balls; cook until brown. Mix the last 4 ingredients in a saucepan and simmer. You may thin with water. Place meatballs in sauce and serve hot. May be prepared a few days before serving or maybe frozen. Make about 6 dozen.

MEATBALLS

Ray Halpin

1½ lb. ground beef
⅓ C. plain breadcrumbs
1 Cloves garlic minced
¼ C. fresh parsley, chopped
1½ T. dried minced onion
¼ C. Parmigiano Reggiano, grated

½ t. Pepper
½ t. Salt
1 Egg

1 T. Fresh Oregano, Chopped, or ½ T. Dried - Fresh is better

Mix all ingredients thoroughly in a large bowl. Cover with plastic wrap and let sit in refrigerator for at least 4 hours. (I make mine the day before and leave it in overnight.). Make whatever size meatballs you'd like. (This recipe makes ~12 meatballs a little larger than a golf ball.). Brown in a frying pan with a little olive on all sides. (You can also bake them to brown), Put in sauce to cook through (~2 hrs).

Appetizers & Beverages

SUPER-PARTY NACHOS

from Jacque's Recipe Box

1 pkg. lean ground turkey
1 pkg. taco seasoning mix
2 tbsp. sliced jalapeno peppers
¼ cup black olives, sliced
1 can black beans, rinsed and drained
1 pkg. tortilla chips
¾ cup water
1 tomato, chopped
1 cup shredded cheese
¼ cup onion, chopped

Brown ground turkey over medium heat. Add taco seasoning and ¾ cup water. Bring to a boil. Reduce heat to low and cook until sauce is thickened (about 5 minutes), stirring occasionally. Arrange thick layer of chips on large microwave-safe plate. Layer with turkey, beans, onion, olives, peppers and cheese. Microwave on high until cheese is melted. Top with tomato. Serve with sour cream, salsa and guacamole.

TURKEY SAUSAGE ROLLS

Earl E. Miller

1 frozen puff pastry sheet   1 lb. frozen turkey sausage meat

Preheat oven to 400°. Thaw pastry for 20 minutes. Thaw turkey sausage meat until able to handle. On a lightly floured surface, roll pastry to a 15½ X 9-inch rectangle. Cut rectangle into 3 strips, 3 inches wide. Divide turkey sausage meat into thirds and roll each into a "snake" the length of the pastry. Place each roll along edge of a pastry strip. Roll the pastry around the turkey sausage meat. Wet edges with ice water and press to seal tightly. Chill the rolls for 1 hour. Cut sausage rolls into ¾-inch slices and place on ungreased baking sheets. Bake for 12 minutes or until pastry is puffed and golden. Serve warm. Makes 60 hors d'oeuvres.

Date Night

Bread & Muffins

CORN MUFFINS

Topeka Ridley

1 cup yellow cornmeal
1 cup flour
¼ cup sugar
3 tsp. baking powder

1 tsp. salt
¼ cup oil
1 cup milk
1 egg, beaten

Preheat oven to 425° F. Combine cornmeal, flour, baking powder and salt in a bowl. Mix oil, egg and milk together and add to dry ingredients; mixing just until batter is uniform. Bake in a greased, 9 x 9 x 2-inch pan for 20-25 minutes for cornbread; or for corn muffins, pour batter into a greased or lined muffin tin (filling about 2/3 full) for 15 to 20 minutes. Makes 12 muffins.

SWEET POTATO BISCUITS

Quiyon Peters

¼ cup sugar
2 tbsp. Milk
3½ cups unbleached all-purpose flour
1½ cups cooked, mashed sweet potatoes
½ cup butter or margarine, melted if potatoes are not hot

1 tsp. salt (opt.)
4½ tsp. baking powder

Heat oven to 425° F. In a large bowl, combine sweet potatoes, butter, sugar and milk; mix well. Into potato mixture, sift flour, baking powder (and salt, if desired). Using a pastry blender, mix well. Using hands, work mixture into a soft dough and chill. Roll or pat dough to ½-inch thickness and cut with a 2½-inch biscuit cutter. Arrange on a greased baking sheet and place on top shelf of oven. Bake for about 15 minutes, until light golden brown. Serve warm. Makes 12 biscuits.

BUTTERMILK BISCUITS (*Tyler Florence*)

Penny Simmons

2 cups all-purpose flour   2 teaspoons baking powder
1 tablespoon sugar   ½ teaspoon baking soda
1 teaspoon salt   ¾ cup buttermilk
½ cup vegetable shortening, chilled, cut into ½-inch pieces

In a mixing bowl, combine dry ingredients together with a fork. Cut in the shortening using a pastry blender until mixture resembles coarse crumbs. Make a well in the center and add buttermilk. Quickly fold dry ingredients into buttermilk with your hands until a sticky dough forms. Turn dough out onto floured surface. Gently fold the dough over itself 3 or 4 times to create layers. Roll dough out to ¾ inch thick. Cut with a 3-inch biscuit cutter. Transfer dough rounds to a sheet pan. Gather scraps and repeat. Make a dimple in the center to help the top rise evenly. Brush with butter. Bake for 15 minutes in a preheated 400° oven until golden brown.

At a friend's wedding

HOECAKE BREAD

Yovonda R. Jones

3 cups all-purpose flour   1 tsp. salt
4 tsp. baking powder   2 tbsp. shortening or vegetable oil
~ ¾ cup water (enough to make a soft, but firm dough)

Combine flour, baking powder and salt. Add shortening and cut through with a butter knife until mixture resembles coarse crumbs. Add enough water to make a dough that is soft, but not sticky. If it is too sticky, just add a little flour, 2 Tbs at a time and knead until mixture is the right consistency. Heat enough melted shortening or vegetable oil to cover the bottom of a large skillet. Form dough into a round ball and divide into 4 equal parts. Form each part into a round ball, then flatten with your hand to form a round, flat bread. Place in hot oil and fry until bottom side is golden brown, then turn over and cook in the same manner until the other side is light brown and the hoecake is puffed up. Repeat for each piece of dough until all are done. Serve with butter and/or jam or jelly. Makes 8.

At Jacque's 60th birthday celebration

HONEY ANGEL BISCUIT

Aunt Eliza Miller

1 pkg. (¼ oz). active dry yeast	1 cup shortening
2 tbsp. warm water (105°-115°)	2 cups buttermilk
5 cups all-purpose flour	tsp. baking soda
1 tsp. salt	1 cup shortening
3 tbsp. honey	Honey Butter

Combine yeast and 2 Tbs. of warm water in a 1-cup measuring cup and let stand for 5 minutes. Combine flour, baking powder, baking soda and salt in a large bowl. Cut in shortening with a pastry blender (or 2 forks) until mixture is crumbly. Combine yeast mixture, buttermilk and honey; add to dry ingredients, stirring until just moistened. Turn dough out onto a lightly floured surface and knead 1 minute. Roll dough to 1/2-inch thickness. Cut with a 2-inch round biscuit cutter and place on ungreased baking sheets. Bake at 400° F for 10 minutes or until golden. Serve with Honey Butter. Makes 5 dozen.

Honey Butter:
½ cup butter or margarine, softened
¼ cup honey

Mix ingredients. Makes 2/3 cups

"God wants us to move out of our limitations and into our possibilities"
Pastor Lawrence Powell

PARKER HOUSE ROLL

Reba Anderson Graham

1 pkg. active dry yeast
3½ to 3¼ cup Gold Medal Flour
¼ cup soft shortening
¼ cup warm water (not hot, 110°-115 °)
¾ cup lukewarm milk (scalded, then cooled)

1 egg
¼ cup sugar
¼ cup salt

In a mixing bowl, dissolve yeast in warm water. Add milk, sugar, egg, shortening and ½ cup of flour. Mix with a spoon until smooth. Add enough remaining flour to handle easily and mix with hand or with spoon. Turn onto a lightly floured, cloth covered board and knead until smooth and elastic, about 5 minutes. Place greased side up in a greased bowl. Cover and let rise in a warm (85°)place until doubled, about 1½ hours. Punch down and let rise again until almost doubled, about 30 minutes. Roll dough ¼-inch thick. Cut with a biscuit cutter and brush with melted butter. Make a crease across with back of knife. Fold so top half slightly overlaps. Press edges together at crease. Place close together on a lightly greased baking sheet. Let rise until light, 15 to 20 minutes. Heat oven to 400° F. Bake for 12 to 15 minutes. Serve hot. Makes about 2 dozen rolls.

*"I will bless the Lord at all times;
His praise shall continually be in my mouth."*

~ Psalm 34:1 (NKJV)

Soup, Stews, Salads & Sauces

*Taste Tester Extraordinaire!
And yes, I loved my mamma's cooking!*

Jacque and I at a backyard picnic in the late 80's, while we were courting.

At lunch in Switzerland

Soup, Stews, Salads & Sauces

FRESH BASIL PESTO (recipe from my late mom, Ann)

Francena Brantley

2 cups fresh basil leaves
½ cup extra virgin olive oil
3 medium size garlic cloves, minced
½ cup freshly grated Parmesan or Romano cheese
Salt and pepper to taste
⅓ cups pine nuts or walnuts

Combine basil and pine nuts in food processor. Pulse a few times. (Nuts should be pulsed a few times before adding basil). Add garlic and pulse a few more times. Slowly add the olive oil with the food processor on. Add grated cheese and pulse until blended. Add salt and pepper to taste. Mom liked to put this in an ice tray and freeze it into cubes. Put in zip lock baggies and use them as needed. Makes about a cup.

POTATO SALAD

Gloria Owens

5 lb. Potatoes
Mayonnaise
1 small jar sweet relish
1/2 cup onion, diced small
celery, diced small
4 eggs
1½ T. French's mustard
1½ T. ketchup
salt, to taste
pepper, to taste
garlic powder, to taste 3/4 cup
Goya Adobo, to taste
1 T. sugar

Put potatoes, with skin on, in a large pot. Add enough water to cover potatoes. Add eggs to pot and boil for 45 minutes to 1 hour. Take potatoes and eggs out of pot and let cool. Peel potatoes and cut into medium-sized cubes, placed in a large bowl. Peel and chop eggs. Add to potatoes. Add salt, pepper, garlic powder and Adobo. Mix, then add ketchup and mustard. Mix again, then add sweet relish, onion, celery, sugar and mayonnaise. Mix well. Season to your taste

DIM SUM DIPPING SAUCE

Roy Halpin

4 T. soy sauce
1 T. Chinese rice vinegar
Mix all ingredients.

1 t. sesame oil
2 t. fresh ginger, minced

BASIC CHINESE HOT SAUCE for STIR FRY

Ray Halpin

¼ C. Rice Wine
1½ T. Oyster Sauce
1 t. Rice Vinegar
2 Scallions
2 t. cornstarch

2 t. Sriracha Chili Sauce
1 clove garlic minced
2 slices fresh ginger minced
A Pinch of sugar

Make the day before and refrigerate overnight. Mix cornstarch in the sauce when you're ready to cook. Stir fry and add the sauce. Sauté until thickened.

MY BBQ SAUCE

Ray Halpin

¼ Cup Brown Sugar
¼ Cup Apple Cider Vinegar
¼ t. Coleman's Dry Mustard
Louisiana Hot Sauce, to taste
A couple splashes of Worcestershire Sauce
1 Cup Water

¼ t. Cayenne Pepper
½ t. Garlic Powder
½ t. Onion Powder
½ Cup Catsup

Mix all ingredients. You can use it as a mop sauce or continue to cook it down to your desired thickness for a finishing sauce.

MARINATED COLLARDS and CABBAGE SALAD
(Recipe from my late mom, Ann)

Francena Brantley

1 small green cabbage
¼ of a small red cabbage
2 cups of collards
1 medium carrot
½ small, sweet onion
½ medium red pepper
* All of the above should be cut in very fine strips.
1 small clove of garlic minced
Cayenne pepper, to taste
Salt, to taste
Pepper, to taste
1   8 oz. bottle of your favorite salad dressing

In large bowl, combine green & red cabbage, collards, carrots, onion, red bell pepper, and garlic. Season to taste with cayenne pepper, salt and pepper. Pour salad dressing over vegetables and toss. Place in refrigerator for 1 hour or more.

You will be elevated to the next level according to the degree you are willing to submit to the authority of another person.

My father was known as the "King of the Grill" because he made his own BBQ sauce and also, a grill from steel drums on which he grilled chicken, pork ribs, beef ribs, and steaks. As you prepare for those special holidays and cookouts, give it a try. (If you have any BBQ goodies left, don't forget where you got the recipe from. I do leftovers).

DADDY'S BARBEQUE SAUCE

Clinton Miller, Jr

2¼ ketchup
½ c. vinegar
½ c. diced, uncooked bacon
¼ c. packed brown sugar
lrg. onion, finely chopped
2½ T. Worcestershire sauce

6 garlic cloves
1 tsp. celery seeds
¾ c. water
¾ tsp. chili powder
½ c. sugar
¾ tsp. red pepper flakes

Combine all ingredients in a Dutch oven or large saucepan. Simmer over low heat for 1½ hours or until sauce is thickened. Cover and store leftover sauce up to 3 days in the refrigerator. Makes 3½ cups.

WILD TURKEY SOUP

Jairus Howell

1 lb. boneless turkey breast	1 bay leaf
salt & pepper to taste	4 med. carrots
1 qt. chicken stock	2 celery stalks, chopped
1 sm. onion, peeled & halved	1 qt. water
1½ c. cooked wild & long grain rice mix	

In a large soup pot, combine the water, chicken stock, onion, celery, bay leaf, salt and pepper. Bring to a rapid boil. Add the turkey breast pieces, reduce heat to low, cover and simmer for 30 minutes or until the meat is tender and cooked through.

Meanwhile, peel and dice the carrots. When the turkey is done, use a slotted spoon to remove it from the stock along with the bay leaf, celery and onion for another use. Allow the turkey to cool slightly and then cut it into cubes. Return the turkey cubes to the stock. Add the cooked wild rice and the diced carrots and return the soup to a boil. Reduce the heat to medium and simmer for another 5 minutes. Serves 6 to 8.

Words of Praise to the Lord:

"I will bless the LORD at all times; His praise shall continually be in my mouth. My soul shall make its boast in the LORD. The humble shall hear of it and be glad. O magnify the LORD, with me. And let us exalt His name together. I sought the LORD and He heard me and delivered me from all my fears."

~ Psalm 34:1-4 N

Clinton and I met in the early 90's as "Promise Keeper Ambassadors" and during an event in which Raleigh Washington spoke. We made an intentional decision to create and maintain a friendship. The Lord has blessed this decision and as Clinton explains this so well, "We are brothers, we have different mothers but the same Father." Love you Brother, God Bless you in the work He has given you to do!

Bob Dell Elba

NEW ENGLAND CLAM CHOWDER (Cheatin Style)

Bob Dell Elba

(Recipe is for two, but you can do the math)
2 cans of Progresso New England Clam Chowder
1 can of whole baby clams
½ stick of butter
Louisiana Hot Sauce (5 drops or to taste)Teaspoon of dried oregano
Teaspoon of dried sweet basilPint of Half and Half cream (Secret Ingredient) 2 full tablespoons of "Old Bay Seasonings"

Cook for 10 minutes or, for larger recipes, cook in Croc Pot for 2 hours. Eat em up with oyster crackers or your favorite toasted bread!

BETTER THAN BASIC CHILI

Ray Halpin

3 lbs. + ground beef
8 Roma tomatoes
1 Lrg. stalk celery
1 Lrg. onion
1 Lrg. clove garlic
1½ C. dried dark red kidney beans
1 mild chili pepper (like an Anaheim)
4 (or more) different kinds of hot peppers (cherry, cayenne, long green, jalapeno as an example)
Salt & pepper to taste
Olive oil
Chili powder
3 cans tomato sauce
1 Bay leaf

Soak kidney beans overnight. In the morning, when you cook the chili, simmer beans in water until tender. Boil approximately 3 quarts of water in a saucepan. Prepare a large bowl with ice water. Dice the onion, celery, and peppers. Mince the garlic. Heat in large pot over low heat with a tablespoon of olive oil. Add a dash of salt and a few turns of pepper. Sweat the vegetables. Do not brown. While that's going, slice a shallow "X" in the skin of each tomato (opposite the stem end). Place them, one or two at a time, in the boiling water for <1 min. Remove them and put into the ice water. Peel and dice the tomatoes. Once the vegetables are wilted, remove them to a bowl. Return the pot to the stove. Add a tablespoon of oil and turn it up to medium heat. Begin browning the ground beef. Do it in batches and drain each batch to remove grease. Don't break it up too much and don't cook it all the way through. Once all the meat is browned, add the meat, vegetables and tomatoes back into the pot. Stir to incorporate. Add the tomato sauce and the bay leaf and stir. Cover the surface of the chili with chili powder and stir. Repeat. Turn down the heat and allow it to simmer with the lid cracked open. Stir occasionally. Drain the kidney beans. After the chili has cooked an hour or so, add the kidney beans to the pot and stir. Cover the pot and turn off. Let it rest for several hours.

Beef, Pork and Lamb

On a cruise with Dr. Myles Monroe

YORKSHIRE BEEF

from Jacque's Recipe Box

1 lb. ground beef	4 oz. shredded cheddar cheese
1 c. (15 oz.) tomato sauce	2 eggs
¼ c. green pepper, chopped	1 c. milk
2 tbsp. flour	1 c. flour
1 tsp. dried parsley flakes	1 tbsp. vegetable oil
½ tsp. salt	2 tbsp. green onions, chopped
½ tsp. pepper	½ tsp. salt

Heat oven to 425°. Cook and stir ground beef in a 10-inch skillet until brown; drain. Stir in tomato sauce, green pepper, 2 tbs. flour, parsley flakes, ½ tsp. salt and pepper. Heat to boil, stirring constantly. Boil and stir for 1 minute. Pour into ungreased 13 x 9 x 2- inch baking pan. Sprinkle with cheese on top. Beat eggs, milk, oil, 1 cup of flour and ½ tsp. salt with hand beater until smooth; pour over cheese. Sprinkle with green onions. Bake until golden brown for 25-30 minutes. Serve immediately.

A Word of Instruction from the Lord:

"He has shown you, O man, what is good; and what does the LORD require of you: But to do justly, to love mercy, and to walk humbly with your God?"

~ Micah 6:8 (NKJV)

RACK OF LAMB

Jeanette S. Miller

1 (1¼ lb.) rack of lamb with at least 8 chops Frenched, well-trimmed & rib bones left long
½ c. fine, fresh breadcrumbs
1½ tsp. finely chopped, fresh rosemary
2 tsp. olive oil
1½ finely chopped garlic
coarse salt & freshly ground pepper
1 T. coarsely chopped, fresh, flat leaf parsley
2 T. Dijon mustard

Preheat oven to 450 degrees with rack in the center. Heat a large cast iron skillet over medium high heat. Rub lamb with the oil and seasoned with salt and pepper. Place in a skillet and sear until golden brown all over, including the ends, about 3 minutes per side. Transfer to a baking sheet and let cool about 30 minutes. In a small bowl, combine breadcrumbs, rosemary, garlic and parsley. Season with salt and pepper. Spread mustard over lamb and cover with an even layer of breadcrumb mixture. Reserve any remaining breadcrumbs for another use. Return to baking sheet and roast until meat thermometer inserted in the thickest part of the meat registers 130° for 20 to 25 minutes. Let stand 5 minutes before serving into individual chops. Serves 8.

"A friend loves at all times, and a brother is born for adversity"
~ Proverbs 17:17

Jacquelyn and I enjoyed traveling to various places around the world from the Caribbean to South Africa. The following recipe was found in a book we bought while visiting South Africa.

BOBOTIE (African Dish)

Clinton Miller, Jr.

1 kg (2 lbs.) minced beef or mutton
1 med. onion, finely chopped
125 ml (½ c.) seedless raisins (opt.)
125 ml (½ c.) blanched almonds (opt.)
12.5 ml (1 T.) apricot jam
12.5 ml (1 T.) fruit chutney
10 ml (2 tsp.) curry powder
10 ml (2 tsp.) salt
1 slice of white bread
10 ml (2 tsp.) butter or oil
3 eggs
250 ml (1 c.) milk
2 lemons or bay leaves
25 ml (2 T.) lemon juice
5 ml (1 tsp.) turmeric

Soak the bread in 125 ml (½ cup) milk. Squeeze to remove the milk and mix the bread with the minced beef. Mix in the raisins, almonds, jam, fruit chutney, curry powder, turmeric and salt. Melt the butter or heat oil in a frying pan and brown the meat mixture lightly in it. Turn out (pour into) a casserole. Beat the eggs and the rest of the milk together and pour over meat. Garnish with bay leaves. Bake in the oven at 350 degrees until set, about 50 minutes. Serves 8

RIB RUB

Ray Halpin

2 tablespoons salt
2 tablespoons brown sugar
1 tablespoon ground cumin
2 tablespoons onion powder
2 tablespoons garlic powder
2 tablespoons freshly ground black pepper
1 tablespoon cayenne pepper
(Could be halved for a less spicy rub)
¼ cup paprika

Mix ingredients. Rub on as much as you'd like the night before. I wouldn't overdo it until you're sure how much you like. Wrap in saran and then foil. Refrigerate until use.

And the Lord will make you the head and not the tail. You shall be above only, and not be beneath, if you heed the commandments of the Lord your God, which I command you today, and are careful to observe them.
~ **Deuteronomy 28:13 (NJKV)**

Seafood, Poultry, Pasta and Casseroles

1st Christmas in our New Home

PASTA SHELLS WITH SMOKED TURKEY

Nicole Miller

8 oz. med. pasta shells (about 3 cups)
¼ tsp. white pepper
1 c. garlic herb cheese spread
8 oz. smoked deli-style turkey or chicken, shredded
1 T. Sweet hot mustard
1 c. fresh Italian parsley
8 oz. smoked deli style turkey or chicken, shredded

In a large pot of boiling, salted water, cook shells to package directions. Drain and reserve 1//2 cup of the cooking water. Return shells and reserved water to pot. Stir in cheese, mustard and pepper until well blended. Add turkey and parsley and toss. Serve immediately. Makes 4 servings.

PORTUGUESE GRILLED CHICKEN

Ray Halpin

1 fryer chicken split in half
Juice of 1 lemon
5 cloves garlic sliced
1 tsp. dried oregano
½ tsp dried thyme
½ tsp. cumin
1 hot peppers
w/seed and ribs removed

1 tsp hot paprika
juice of 1 lime: zest of half
splash of rice wine vinegar
¼ chicken broth
½ tsp. salt
½ tsp. pepper
½ tsp. sugar

Marinate chicken for 4 hours (overnight is better). Start with skin side down and grill on medium low heat for 30 min. Flip and cook until juices run clear (another 15-30 min).

Seafood, Poultry, Pasta and Casseroles

RICE AND CHICKEN

from Jacque's Recipe Box

3 Tbsp. olive oil
3 cloves of garlic, minced
¾ cup green pepper, diced
2 chicken bouillon cubes
4-6 pieces of chicken, seasoned with salt and pepper

3 cups water
1 cup onions, diced
1 8 oz. can tomato sauce
1½ cups parboiled rice

Over medium heat, heat oil in a large pot and sauté chicken pieces until brown. Add minced garlic and sauté with chicken for about 2 minutes. Add onion and green pepper and cook for about 5 minutes until vegetables are tender. Stir in tomato sauce and bouillon cubes. Add water and bring to a boil. Add rice and stir. Reduce heat to low and cover. Cook for 25 minutes or until rice istender. Serves 4.

TURKEY SAUSAGE, PEPPERS AND ONIONS

from Jacque's Recipe Box

1 pkg. (approx. 1 lb.) Italian turkey sausage, hot or sweet
3 Tbsp. olive oil
2 cups onion, cut in strips
1 red bell pepper, cut in strips
1 green bell pepper, cut in strips
1 clove garlic, crushed

Place sausage links in a large skillet filled with 1/4-inch water. Cover and simmer 8-10 minutes. Uncover and cook until liquid is absorbed, and sausages are browned. Transfer to a side dish. Heat oil in same skillet; add onions, peppers and garlic; sauté 2 minutes. Add sausage, cover and cook over low heat for 10 minutes, stirring occasionally. If desired, serve with toasted bread

SAN FRANCISCO CHICKEN – DECONSTRUCTED

Ray Halpin

4 chicken breasts pounded thin (~ ¼ in.) 1 French Roll
¼ c. Fresh Parsley   1 Clove Garlic
1 T. Parmigiano Reggiano
1 T. Hot Hungarian Paprika

Cut roll in half and bake in oven at 225° until stale (about 20 min.) Cut roll into chunks and put in food processor along with parsley and cheese. Process until relatively fine crumbs. Add paprika, garlic and a dash of salt & pepper. Mix to combine. Spread flour on waxed paper. Add a dash of salt & pepper. Put egg whites in a bowl. Spread breadcrumbs on waxed paper. Dust chicken in flour. Pat off excess. Dip in egg whites. Dip in breadcrumbs to coat uniformly. Put on rack in refrigerator until ready to fry. Melt butter and oil in a heavy skillet. Place chicken in pan when oil is about 350°. Do in batches. Cook on each side until golden brown. Remove to rack, drizzle with a little lemon juice and place in oven on 200° to hold, if necessary. Serve with corn on the cob and sliced tomatoes.

John and Barbara Sidney have been friends of ours for over 30 years. We were in each other's wedding. John and I had managed to stay two cool single dudes until Barbara and Jacquelyn caught our attention. After that, it was a wrap, and the rest is history.

TURKEY MEATLOAF

John B. Sidney

2 lbs. ground turkey
1 tsp. black pepper
2 eggs, beaten
½ tsp. salt
1 c. rolled oats
½ tsp. basil
½ c. chopped onion
½ tsp. garlic powder
½ c. ketchup
3 T. packed brown sugar
2 T. steak sauce
1 tsp. ground mustard
¼ c. chopped green pepper

Preheat oven to 350° and grease an 8½ inch loaf pan. In a large bowl, combine the ground turkey and eggs. Add the oats, onion, ketchup, green pepper, steak sauce, black pepper, salt, basil and garlic powder and mix well. Transfer to the loaf pan and smooth the top. In a small bowl, whisk the ketchup, brown sugar and mustard together, then spread it over the meatloaf before baking. Bake for 1 to 1½ hours or until the inside reaches 160°. Let meatloaf sit for 10 minutes before slicing. Serves 4-6.

SAN FRANCISCO CHICKEN BREASTS

Ray Halpin

3 or 4 chicken breasts, boned and skinned
¾ cup dry breadcrumbs*
¾ cup grated Parmesan cheese*
3 T. finely chopped parsley*
2 tsp salt*
¼ tsp white pepper

12 T. butter or margarine (I use some butter and olive oil)
1 clove garlic (I use lots)
2 lemons

I have taken to buying Italian seasoned breadcrumbs and adding the cheese, even if there is cheese in the mixture. Preheat the oven to 350° F. Split each chicken breast and pepper well. (I pound them a bit to even out the cooking). Blend the breadcrumbs, cheese, parsley and salt with a fork. (Unless you're using seasoned crumbs). Melt the butter and press the garlic into it. Simmer gently for 3 minutes. (I do this in the microwave for less time). Dip each piece of chicken into the butter and then into the bread crumb mixture. Roll each piece up tightly and fasten it with a toothpick or small skewer. Place in a buttered baking dish. I bake them on a cookie sheet on a rack. Sprinkle the chicken liberally with lemon juice, the remaining butter and a dash of paprika. Bake 1 hour. While still hot, remove the toothpicks. Hard to get out when cold, for leftovers.

*"Oh, taste and see that the LORD is good;
blessed is the man who trusts in Him."*

~ Psalm 34:8

GROUND TURKEY SKILLET CASSEROLE

Barbara Sidney

Vegetable oil spray
¾ tsp. salt
2 T. sugar
1 lb. ground turkey
T. low sodium Worcestershire Sauce
1 med. green pepper, finely chopped
6 oz. dried, no yolk egg noodles
10 oz. frozen mixed vegetables
¼ c. snipped, fresh parsley
1 (8 oz.) can no salt added tomato sauce
½ T. dried Italian seasoning, crumbled

Heat a 12-inch, non-stick skillet over medium heat. Remove from heat and lightly spray with vegetable oil spray. Do not spray near gas flame. Cook ground turkey for 3 minutes or until browned, stirring frequently. Pour into a colander and rinse under hot water to remove excess fat. Drain well. Wipe skillet with paper towels. Return ground turkey to skillet. Stir in bell pepper and cook for 3 minutes or until just tender and crisp, stirring frequently. Stir in mixed vegetables, tomato sauce, Worcestershire sauce, Italian seasoning and sugar. Bring to a boil over medium-high heat. Reduce heat and simmer covered for 20 minutes or until green beans in mixed vegetables are tender. Meanwhile, prepare noodles using package directions, omitting salt and oil. Drain well, reserving ¾ cups of cooking water. Stir noodles, reserved water, parsley and salt into ground turkey mixture. Serves 4 (1½ cup) servings.

CHICKEN, SHRIMP & ANDOUILLE JAMBALAYA

Ray Halpin

1 T. Unsalted Butter	Salt and Pepper
1 Andouille Sausage, Sliced	Parsley for garnish
1 Med. Onion, Diced	1 Bay Leaf
1 Cup Plain Tomato Sauce	½ t. Dried Thyme
1 Stalk Celery, Diced	1 t. Kosher Salt
4 Cloves Garlic, Minced	¾ t. White Pepper
2 Plum Tomatoes, Diced	½ t. Cayenne
¾ Cup Enriched Long Grain Rice	1 Cup Chicken Stock
12 Large Shrimp, Peeled & Deveined	5 Chicken Thighs
1 Bell Pepper, Diced	

(I prefer a mildly hot pepper – Anaheim chili)

Preheat oven to 350°. Melt the butter over medium heat in a large skillet. Sauté the Andouille until slightly browned. Add onion, celery and bell pepper with a little salt & pepper and sauté until tender. Add garlic, sauté for about a minute. Add diced tomatoes and sauté for about a minute. Add the tomato sauce, cook a minute more. Add the rice and cook for a minute. Add the stock, cayenne, white pepper, salt, thyme, bay leaf and raw chicken thighs. Stir well and put in oven. Bake uncovered for about 30-40 minutes, or until the rice is cooked. At about 25 minutes, remove the thighs and debone, coarsely chop the meat and return to the skillet Nestle the shrimp into the rice and return the skillet to the oven. When rice and shrimp are done, you're done. Garnish with parsley.

Desserts, Pies, Cakes and Cookies

May 15, 2001, when Jacque received her Master's degree in School Counseling from New Jersey City University

Desserts, Pies, Cakes and Cookies

OLD-FASHIONED PLAIN CAKE

Jo Ann Pringle

1 cup butter
2 cups sugar
3 cups flour
6 eggs

½ tsp. salt
1 tsp. vanilla
1 cup buttermilk
3 tsp. baking powder

Heat oven to 350° F. Cream butter, salt and sugar until light. Beat eggs and add to creamed mixture, blending well. Sift flour and baking powder together. Add alternately with buttermilk and beat well for 5 minutes. Bake in greased layer pans or a loaf pan until done (20 to 30 minutes for layer cake, 45 to 60 minutes for loaf). Layer and ice cakes as desired.

EASY LEMON POUND CAKE

Mary Green

1 box lemon cake mix (any brand)
1 pkg. lemon Jell-O
¾ cups corn oil
Icing:
½ can of lemon concentrate frozen juice (unthaw)
2 Tbsp. of butter melted
1½ cups of powdered sugar

3 eggs
¾ cups water
1 tsp. lemon extract

Mix all ingredients for cake together. Pour into greased and floured bunt pan. Bake at 350° for 40-45 minutes. Icing: Mix all ingredients for icing together. When cake is done & cooled enough to take out of bunt pan, immediately pour icing over warm cake. Let cake soak up icing.

OLD FASHIONED APPLE CRISP (recipe from my late mom, Ann)

Francena Brantley

½ tsp. Cinnamon
¼ cup sugar

1 tsp. flour
4-5 cups sliced apples

Topping:
1 cup sugar
1 cup flour
1 tsp. baking powder

1 egg beaten

¼ lb. melted butter

Combine cinnamon, sugar & flour. Toss with sliced apples. Put in greased 8" square pan. Topping: Stir sugar, flour & baking powder together. Mix in egg with a fork until crumbly. Sprinkle over apples. Pour melted butter over all. Bake at 375° for 45 minutes. Serve plain or with whipped cream.

SWEET POTATO POUND CAKE (recipe from my late mom, Ann)

Francena Brantley

1 box yellow cake mix
½ cup oil
¾ cup sugar
¼ cup water

4 eggs
1 tsp. cinnamon
1 cup mashed sweet potatoes

Frosting:
1   stick margarine, softened
1 8 oz. pkg. cream cheese, softened

1 tsp. vanilla

Grease & flour bundt pan. Preheat oven to 350°. Combine all ingredients for cake and mix well. Pour in pan and bake for 1 hour. Remove from pan, cool and frost.

Desserts, Pies, Cakes and Cookies

CREAM CHEESE POUND CAKE

Jacqueline McNeil

2 sticks of butter, unsalted
2 cups sugar
8 oz. package Cream cheese, room temperature
2¼ cups Self-Rising Flour, sifted
6 large eggs or jumbo (jumbo makes it really moist)
½ Tbsp. vanilla & lemon flavor (I am not too sure about this one. I don't measure, I just judge)

Mix butter & cream cheese together. Add sugar. Add flour. Add eggs. Add flavor. Preheat oven to 350° F. Spray cake pan with PAM or oil and coat with flour, then add cake batter. Bake at 350° for 45 minutes or until golden brown and cake starts to separate from the sides of the cake pan; test with toothpick at center of cake, if toothpick is clean, the cake is ready to take out. Enjoy!

"This Book of the Law shall not depart from your mouth, but you shall meditate in it day and night, that you may observe to do according to all that is written in it. For then you will make your way prosperous, and then you will have good success. Have I not commanded you? Be strong and of good courage; do not be afraid, nor be dismayed, for the Lord your God is with you wherever you go."

~ Joshua 1:8-9 (NKJV)

Desserts, Pies, Cakes and Cookies

PECAN GLAZED PUMPKIN PIE

Tonique Moore

2 eggs
1 can (16 oz.) Pumpkin
1 cup brown sugar, divided
1 can (12 oz.) evaporated milk
1 deep dish or 2 regular pie crust shells

1 cup pecan pieces
2 tsp. pumpkin pie spice
2 Tbsp. butter, melted

Preheat oven and baking sheet to 375° F. In large bowl, using a wire whisk, whisk together eggs, pumpkin, evaporated milk, ¾ cup sugar and pumpkin pie spice. Re-crimp edge of deep-dish crust only to stand ½ inch above rim. Place frozen pie crust on preheated baking sheet. Pour filling into crust. Bake 30 minutes (20 minutes for regular crust). In small bowl, combine remaining ¼ cup sugar, pecans and melted butter. Crumble over top of partially baked pie. Bake an additional 20 to 30 minutes, or until knife inserted in center comes out clean. Yields 8 servings (12 with regular crust).

"Trust in the Lord with all your heart and lean not on your own understanding; in all your ways acknowledge Him, and He shall direct your paths."
~ Proverbs 3:5-6 (NJKV)

Desserts, Pies, Cakes and Cookies

OLD FASHIONED POUND CAKE (recipe from my late mom, Ann)
Francena Brantley

2 cups butter softened
2¾ cups sugar
6 large eggs
⅛ tsp. salt
¼ tsp. ground nutmeg
½ cup milk

Beat butter at medium speed with an electric mixer for about 3 minutes or until soft and creamy. Gradually add sugar and beat at medium speed for 5 to 7 minutes. Add one egg at a time and beat until yellow disappears. In a separate bowl combine flour, salt and nutmeg. Add to creamed mixture alternating with milk. Begin with and end with flour mixture. Mix at low speed until blended. After each addition stir in vanilla. Pour batter into greased and floured 10" tube pan. Bake at 325° for 1 hr. 15 or 20 minutes or until toothpick comes out clean. Cool in pan or on a wire rack 10 to 15 minutes. Remove from pan, let cool completely on rack.

BROWNIES
Tanari Ridley

½ cup unsweetened cocoa powder
¾ cup granulated sugar
½ cup cake flour, sifted
Tbs. unsweetened applesauce
1 Tbs, chopped walnuts or pecans
1 large egg
2 Tbs. vegetable oil
1-½ tsp. vanilla extract
¼ tsp. salt
2 egg whites

Preheat oven to 350° F. Spray an 8-inch, square baking pan with vegetable cooking spray and set aside. In a medium bowl, combine flour, cocoa and salt; mix well. In a large bowl, whisk together egg whites, egg, sugar applesauce, oil and vanilla. Stir in flour mixture until just blended. Do not over mix. Pour batter into prepared pan and sprinkle with nuts. Bake until just set and a toothpick inserted in the center comes out clean (about 25 minutes). Place pan on a wire rack and cool for at least 15 minutes. Cut brownies into squares and place on a serving plate. Makes 12 squares.

LEMON CHEESE PIE

Penny Simmons

1 (9 inch) graham cracker crumb crust
1 (8 oz.) pkg. cream cheese, softened
1 (14 oz.) can Condensed Milk
⅓ cup lemon juice (from concentrate)
1 tsp. vanilla extract

Lemon Topping:
⅓ cup sugar   ¼ cup lemon juice
2½ tsp. cornstarch   ½ cup water
¼ cup lemon juice   1 egg
yolk 1 Tbsp. butter or margarine

In mixing bowl, beat cream cheese until fluffy. Gradually beat in condensed milk until smooth. Stir in lemon juice and vanilla extract. Pour into crust. Top with lemon topping. Chill 3 hours. Garnish as desired.

For topping: In saucepan, combine ⅓ cup sugar and 2½ tsp. cornstarch. Add ½ cup water, ¼ cup lemon juice and 1 egg yolk; mix well. Over medium heat, cook and stir until thickened. Remove from heat; stir in 1 Tbs. butter or margarine until melted.

CHOCOLATE PEANUT BUTTER BROWNIES

Guy A. Holley

1 - 15.5 oz can of black beans, drained and rinsed well
1 large egg
2 large egg whites
3 tsp. pure vanilla extract
2/3 cup Truvia baking formula or 1½ cup of sugar
¼ cup melted butter
½ cup unsweetened cocoa powder
⅓ cup semisweet or dark chocolate chips
4 Tbsp. all-natural peanut butter

Preheat oven to 350°. Spray and 8 x 8- inch pan with cooking spray. Blend all ingredients (except butter and 2 Tbs. of Peanut Butter) in a food processor or powerful blender until very well blended. You may need to scrape the sides and blend again. When it's just about finished processing, add in the melted butter. Then stir in the chocolate chips by hand. Spread into the prepared pan. Swirl in the remaining peanut butter into the top of the batter. Bake for 25-30 minutes until set around the outside and in the middle. It will just start to crack. Don't test with a toothpick, as it won't come out clean. You want them to be fudge-like anyway! Cool completely and cut into 16 squares. Store in an airtight container in the fridge.

*"Where I am is not who I am
because who I am is greater than where I am"*

Dr. Samuel Chan

CARAMELIZED APPLE CAKE

Jo Ann Pringle

2 large Granny Smith apples, peeled, cored and cut into ¾ inch slices
½ cup packed dark brown sugar
1½ tsp. baking powder
⅔ cup granulated sugar
½ cup (1 stick) plus 5 Tbsp. unsalted butter, softened

2 eggs
½ tsp. salt
½ cup sour cream
1 tsp. vanilla extract
1½ cup flour

Heat oven to 375°. Mix flour, baking powder and salt in a medium size bowl. Set aside. Using an electric mixer on high speed, beat ½ cup of the butter in a large bowl for 1 minute or until creamy. Add granulated sugar and continue to beat until light and fluffy. Add eggs and vanilla and beat until blended. Reduce speed to low. Gradually blend in flour mixture, then sour cream. Melt remaining 5 Tbs. of butter in an ovenproof, 10-inch, nonstick skillet. Add brown sugar and stir 2 minutes. Add apple slices to the pan and reduce heat to medium-low. Cook for about 10 minutes or until tender. Let cool for 5 minutes. Spoon batter over apples and spreadedge to edge of pan. Bake at 375° F for 30 minutes or until goldenbrown. Cool on a rack for 20 minutes. Run a knife around edge ofpan and carefully invert cake onto a plate. Makes 10 servings.

COCONUT POUND CAKE

Jackie M. Ridley

½ c. flaked coconut
3 c. all-purpose flour
¼ c. powdered sugar
1 tsp. baking powder
1 c. butter, softened
1 c. milk

½ c. butter flavored shortening
2 T. coconut flavoring
3 c. sugar
1 tsp. vanilla
5 eggs, room temp

Heat oven to 325°. Grease a 10-inch (16-cup) tube pan. Line the bottom of pan with foil or parchment paper. Grease foil and flour pan. In a small bowl, stir together coconut and powdered sugar until coconut is well coated. Evenly sprinkle over bottom of pan. In a large bowl, beat butter and shortening at medium-high speed for 1 minute or until fluffy. Beat in sugar 3 to 4 minutes or until light and fluffy. Beating at low speed, add eggs one at a time, beating well after each addition. In a medium bowl, stir together flour and baking powder. Alternately beat flour mixture and milk into butter mixture just until incorporated, beginning and ending with flour mixture. Beat in coconut flavoring and vanilla. Pour into pan and bake for 1 hour and 45 minutes or until a wooden skewer inserted in the center comes out clean. Cool in pan on a wire rack 20 minutes. Invert cake onto wire rack, remove pan and foil. Cool completely. Some coconut tipping may stick to foil. Remove with a fork and arrange over top of cake. Serves 12.

BROKEN GLASS TORTE (recipe from late mom, Ann)

Francena Brantley

It looks like a stained-glass window!

1 pkg. each of 3 different Jell-O's
1½ cups boiling water
1½ pkg. Knox unflavored gelatin
1 cup hot pineapple juice

½ cup sugar
¼ cup cold water
1 tsp. vanilla
2 cups heavy cream

CRUST
½ cup soft butter (¼ lb.)
1½ cups crushed graham cracker crumbs

½ cup sugar

Dissolve 1 pkg. each of three different Jell-O's in 1½ cups boiling water for each package. (Mom used 4 different kinds of Jell-O, taking off ¼ of each color. Combination of two dark, such as grape and strawberry, then a lime and either an orange or a lemon is nice. Chill in separate cake pans until firm. Then cut into cubes or steps about ½ inch wide. Soften 1½ pkg. Knox unflavored gelatin in ¼ cup cold water and then dissolve in 1 cup hot pineapple juice. Let cool. Whip 2 cups heavy cream. Add ½ cup sugar and 1 tsp. vanilla. Fold juice mixture into whipped cream mixture and carefully blend colored Jell-O cubes into mixture of both. Pour into spring form pan lined with ⅔ graham cracker crust. Sprinkle remaining ⅓ of crumbs on top and chill overnight for best results.

Crust: Combine all ingredients together in a bowl.

Desserts, Pies, Cakes and Cookies

PEACH COBBLER

Filling: *Aunt Eliza Miller*

2½ lbs. fresh peaches
½ cup sugar
Topping:
1½ cups all-purpose flour
¾ tsp. baking powder
¼ tsp. baking soda
⅓ cup reduced-fat sour cream
1 egg, lightly beaten for glazing
1 Tbs. chilled butter, cut into small pieces

2 Tbsp. all-purpose flour
1 Tbsp. fresh lemon juice

2 Tbsp. sugar
½ tsp. salt
1½ Tbsp. canola oil
3 to 4 Tbsp. 1 % milk

Preheat oven to 375º F. Lightly oil a shallow, 2½ to 3-quart baking dish or coat it with nonstick spray. Using a slotted spoon, dip peaches in a large pot of boiling water for 30 to 40 seconds. Let cool briefly, then peel off skins. Halve, pit and thickly slice peaches. In a large bowl, combine sugar, flour and cinnamon. Add peaches and lemon juice; toss to coat. Transfer to prepared pan. **Topping:** In a medium bowl, combine flour, 1 Tbs. sugar, baking powder, salt and baking soda. Work in oil and butter with your fingers until coarse crumbs form. In a large bowl whisk sour cream and milk. Add flour mixture and stir with a fork just until dough forms. On a lightly floured surface, knead several times until smooth. On a sheet of waxed paper, dust dough with flour and pat into a disk. Cover with another sheet of waxed paper and roll out ½ inch smaller than the baking dish. Peel off top sheet of paper. Invert dough onto filling and peel off paper. Cut several slashes in dough to vent steam. Brush top lightly with egg and sprinkle with remaining 1 Tbsp. of sugar. Bake cobbler for 35 to 40 minutes or until top is browned. Filling should be bubbling, and a toothpick inserted in the center of the topping comes out clean. Cool for at least 10 minutes. Serve warm. Makes 8 servings.

Forever Love

My First Love

She's gone. She left me for another man.

Jacquelyn left me for someone who loved her more than I did, gave her more than I could have ever thought of giving her, and loved her in ways that I could never even think of, much less imagine.

Right in front of me, while I stood there next to her, Jacquelyn would tell Him how much she loved Him. It never bothered her for people to know her love for Him. Openly and overtly, she would tell anybody and everybody about her "First Love."

My wife cared for me and told me so, but if He called, she would leave me and go to Him for as long as He wanted to be with her. There were times in her last few months when she would longingly call unto Him, wanting to be with Him, all the time knowing that I understood.

Hers was a lifetime love affair with Him. I could never compete with this Man, and I didn't even try. Jacquelyn loved Him passionately, and I was never jealous because I realized it helped her to love me with passion.

There were times when I would suddenly come upon her in her secret place loving Him through praise and worship; I would tiptoe away so as not to interfere with her prayer time with Him. He came first; therefore, I gladly and willingly accepted my secondary role in her life. Her "First Love" really came first in every sense of the word.

Jacquelyn would read His love letters to her which He had written in a Book and would quote passages to me. I often wrote her love letters but mine seemed so anemic and weak compared to His letters. Only when I quoted some of His passages did they seem to take on life and meaning.

There was never a day in her life when she did not meet with Him. There were even times when she spent hours with Him telling Him about other people's needs who were asking for help. Some of these individuals she had never met or would ever meet, but she knew He cared for them and desired to meet their every need.

Jacquelyn spent time sharing the most intimate details of her life with this Man. Some of the information she never shared with anyone else except Him, because she believed that He understood her.

One night, as I held her in my arms, Jacquelyn told me that she was going to leave me. I cried so hard she could hardly comfort me. I learned to trust her completely when she spoke those words to me. I realized she wanted to be relieved from the pain caused by the disease of cancer that had overtaken her body.

She assured me that her "First Love" would deliver her from the pain and discomfort that she had been experiencing. This Man gave Jacquelyn His Word He would never leave her nor forsake her, and He kept His Word. Having loved her so dearly, He loved her unto the end.

The name of her "First Love" is JESUS!

I affectionately called Jacquelyn, "Sweetheart" because she was a lady of love. All who knew her, loved her, and those she knew, she loved. Without a doubt, she was a Wife of Noble Character: "Charm is deceptive, and beauty is fleeting; but a woman who fears the LORD is to be praised." (Proverbs 31:30 NIV).

Jacquelyn was my lady, my lover, and my best friend!

Affectionately yours,
Clinton Miller Jr

Isn't she lovely? Isn't she beautiful?...

Taken from Jacque's Bible

"Clinton officially asked me to marry him at 9:50 PM on July 10, 1990. We had left church and were riding down Flatbush Ave. Of course, I accepted. Hallelujah! We were following Pastor Bernard en route to Junior's for a late dinner meeting."

Taken from notes written in Jacque's Bible, before I proposed...

May 4, 1990
1 Sam 15:29

"God said He is not a man that He should lie. He has given Clinton to me as a gift. He has not changed His mind."

Taken from notes written in Jacque's Bible, after I proposed...

August 28, 1990
2 Cor 1:21-22

"It is this God who has made you and me into faithful Christians and commissioned us apostles to preach the Good News. He has put his brand upon us - his mark of ownership - and given us his Holy Spirit in our hearts as a guarantee that we belong to him and as the first installment of all that he is going to give us."

"Hallelujah! What is this brand? Is it love? Discuss with Clinton".

Jacque and I truly liked, loved and respected one another. Our relationship was built on trust and communication. We had prayer and devotion every day before we got married, so praying for each other after we were married was natural for us. I treated her the way she deserved to be treated so that the only man she would ever leave me for is the only man who could ever love her more than me… Jesus.

It is my firm belief that every marital relationship should be built on trust and communication. Both the husband and the wife should be willing to forgive each other unconditionally, sacrificially, and redemptively as Christ has forgiven us. There should also be a willingness on the part of each partner to seek godly counsel when needed, as well as positive, healthy relationships with other couples who are striving to make their marriage the best that it can be.

Your marriage should be comprised of a three-some: husband, wife, and the Lord. The Bible says, " A three-fold cord is not easily broken."

On our Honeymoon, May 21,

AFWC Women's Fellowship Retreat at Sandy Cove

Miscellaneous

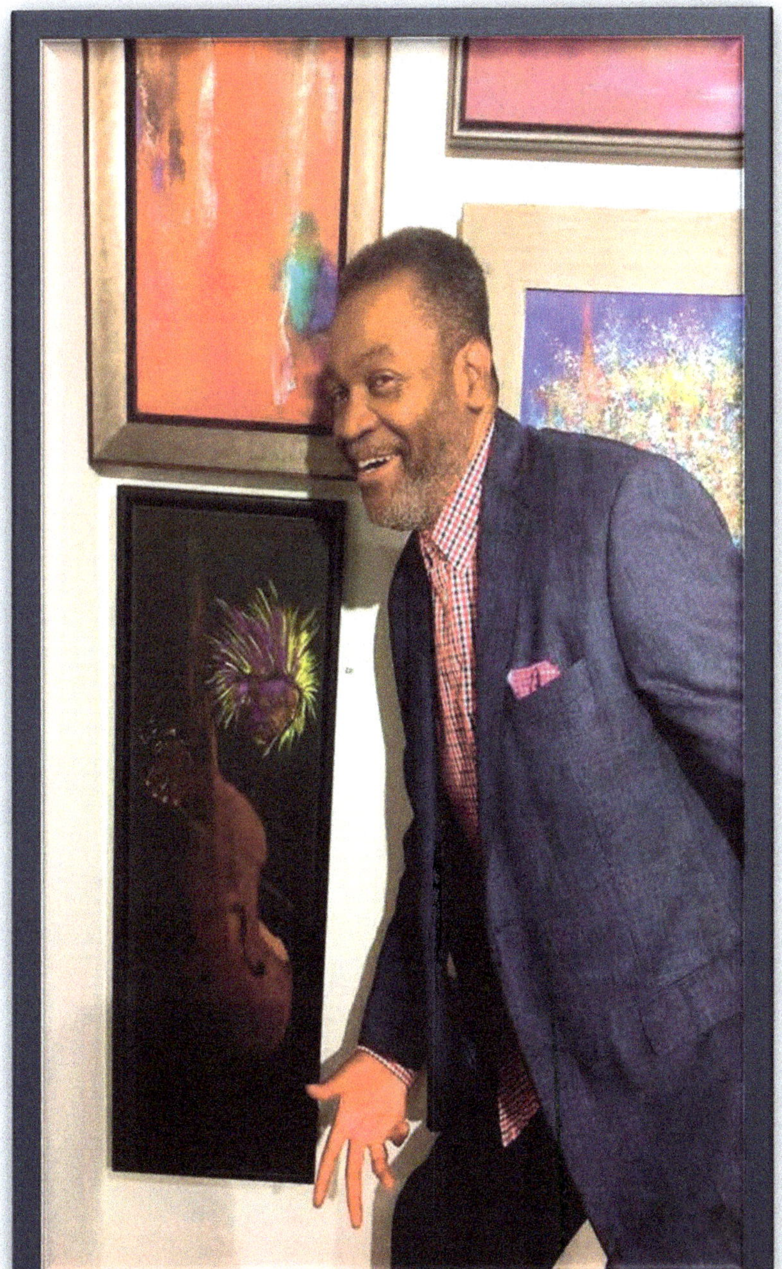

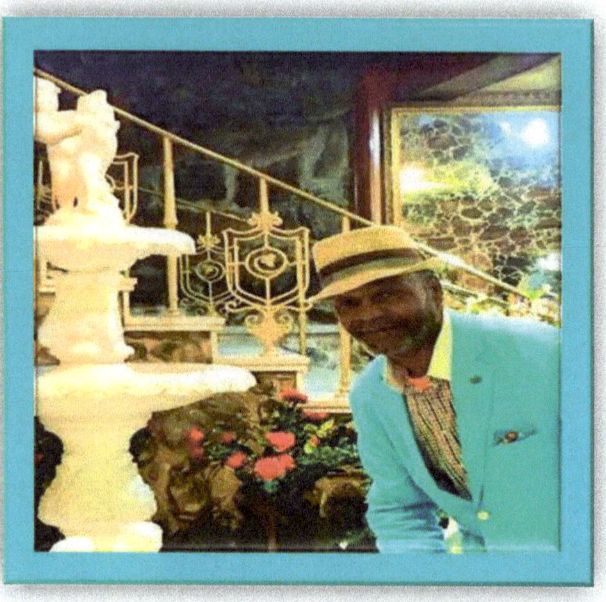

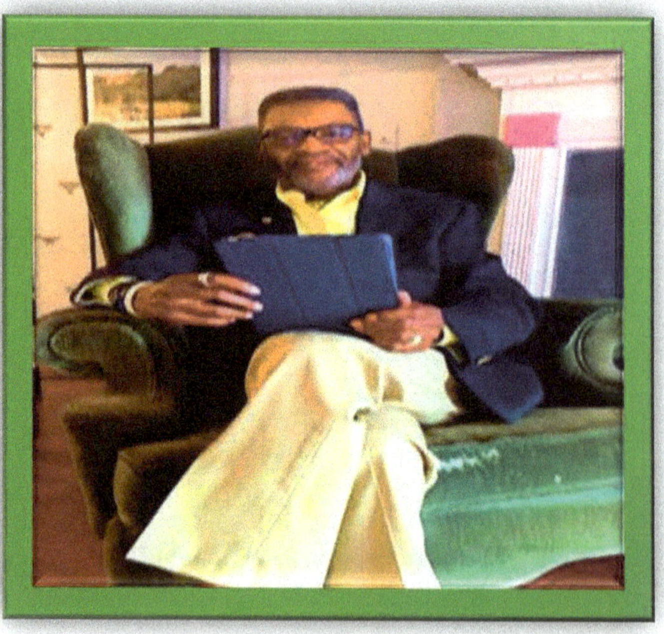

Vegetables & Side Dishes

Vegetables and Side Dishes

CORN PUDDING (Mrs. Era S. Loyd)

Derek Peters

4 ears white corn
4 eggs
¾ c. canned milk

salt and black pepper to taste
2 Tbsp. sugar to taste
1 stick butter or margarine

Cut off corn from ears twice; do not scrape cob. Add all other ingredients; mix well. Grease 1¼ quart Pyrex dish with butter or margarine; pour in corn mixture. Place Pyrex dish in a shallow pan of water and bake in preheated 400° oven. Let bake for 15 minutes and then beat with a fork. Bake for 45 minutes or until firm; do not over bake. Serve hot. Serves 6 to 8.

FRIED OKRA

from Jacque's Recipe Box

1 lb. okra
8 cups water
¼ cup salt

½ cup cornmeal
vegetable oil for frying

Wash okra and drain well. Cut off the tips and stems and cut into ½ inch slices. Combine the water and salt and pour over the okra in a large saucepan. Bring to a boil then reduce heat to simmer for 15 minutes. Drain and rinse well. In a large skillet, bring the oil to frying temperature. Roll the okra in cornmeal and fry in the hot oil. Yields 6 servings.

HOT AND SPICY COLLARD GREENS

Lititiah D. Youman

5 lbs. fresh collard greens, stems removed & sliced
½ lb. ham, shredded or diced
2 T. vegetable oil
4 pickled jalapeño peppers
Lg, onion chopped
3 garlic cloves, minced
2 T.sugar
2 to 3 c. water

Soak greens in several changes of cold water to remove all grit. Remove and discard tough stems. In bunches, stack, roll and slice crosswise into 1-inch-wide strips. In a large pot, heat oil and sauté onion and garlic. Stir in water, ham, jalapeño peppers and sugar. Simmer for about 1 to 1½ hours. Serves 12.

Bitter or better, which one will you be?
The difference is just one letter, you see…Take the "i" out of bitter and replace it with "e" and things will be better for you and for me.

Do you know Him?

For God so loved the world, that He gave His only begotten Son, that whosoever believeth in Him should not perish, but have everlasting life.

~ John 3:16 (KJV)

"How beautiful on the mountains are the feet of the messenger who brings good news, the good news of peace and salvation, the news that the God of Israel reigns!"

~ Isaiah 52:7 (LB)

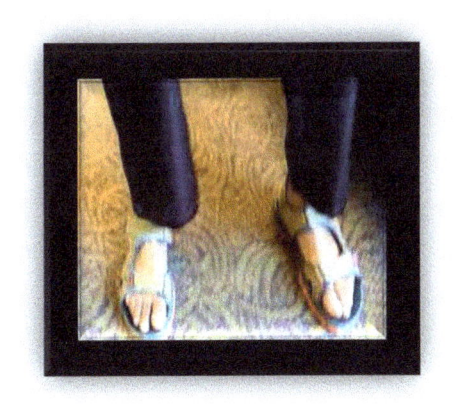

Clinton Miller, Jr.
cmillerjr122@gmail.com

About the Author

Clinton Miller, Jr is a passionate educator and counselor who has invested over fifty years imparting unique teaching and counseling skills into countless students, emphasizing the importance of interpersonal relationships and self-worth.

Born in Newark, NJ, and raised in a small Georgia town, Clinton received nurturing and a strong sense of family and love from his maternal grandmother, Claudia Wooten West. *Big Mama,* as Mrs. Claudia West was affectionately called, had a profound impact on Clinton's childhood development and maturity. She introduced him to a love of food and cooking at a young age while assisting her in a warm, southern kitchen. Big Mama brought Clinton to a local Baptist church where he accepted Jesus Christ as his Lord and Savior which was the beginning of his Christian walk.

Miss Claudia instilled a strong sense of family, honesty, integrity, character and an appreciation of learning and education into Clinton's life at an early age. Because of his love for learning and teaching, Clinton majored in education and began his teaching career with the Elizabeth Board of Education School District after graduating from Kean University (formally Newark State College in 1968 where he received both a Bachelor of Arts in Elementary Education and a Master's degree in Behavioral Sciences). In addition, he received Substance Awareness Coordinator and General Theological Studies Certificates in 1994 and 2009 respectively.

In May of 2012, Clinton Miller Jr. attended Cairn University in Langhorne PA where he received his Master of Science Degree in Christian Counseling. He is an active Core Team Member of the Higher Standards Singles Ministry at Agape Family Worship Center, Rahway, NJ, as well as a member/Mentor of the International Christian Brotherhood (ICB). In addition, he serves on numerous men's mentoring programs and community organizations throughout Central New Jersey. He is also an active Board of Directors member for Prevention Links of Union County in Roselle. NJ.

During the summers of 2014/2015, he participated in a Summer Teaching Program (STP) in cooperation with the English Language Institute in China (ELIC) where he taught English to Chinese/ English teachers. He was also assigned as an Instructor/Tutor to Chinese Scholars at Rutgers University in New Brunswick, NJ from the 2015 school year to 2020. In April 2017, Mr. Miller was ordained as a Minister of the Gospel at Agape Family Worship Center, Rahway, NJ. Since March 2016, he has been a Student Advisor at Union County College, Cranford, NJ Campus.

After forty years of an adventurous, enjoyable, and exciting teaching life experience, he retired from the school district in 2008. Indeed, the gift of Clinton Miller, Jr. is that his entire life personifies one of a love for education, learning and humanity.

Cooking terms

Baste - To moisten foods during cooking with pan drippings or special sauce to add flavor and prevent from drying out.

Beat - Stir together very rapidly to incorporate air. This can be achieved with a spoon, whisk, electric mixer, or food processor.

Blend - Stir ingredients together until well mixed..

Blanche - To immerse in rapidly boiling water for a short time.

Caramelize - To heat a sugar substance until it begins to turn brown

Cream – Beat together sugar and butter until a light, creamy texture and color has been achieved. Sometimes eggs are also added during the creaming step.

Cut In – Incorporating butter (or another solid fat) into flour just until the fat is in small, granular pieces resembling coarse sand.

Dredge - To coat lightly with flour or cornmeal.

Fold - To add a delicate substance, such as whipped cream or beaten eggs into another substance using a spatula to gently bring part the mixture from the bottom of the bowl to the top. Repeating the process until all the ingredients is thoroughly mixed.

Glaze - To coat with a thick sugar-based sauce

Grease – Coat the inside of a baking dish or pan with a fattysubstance (oil, butter, lard) to prevent sticking.

Knead – Combine dough by hand on a hard surface. This involves folding the dough over, pressing down, turning 90 degrees and then repeating the process.

Marinate - To allow food to soak in a seasoned liquid.

Mince – To chop food into very small pieces.

Sauté – The process to cook and/or brown food quickly in a small amount of cooking oil in a skillet over direct heat.

Simmer - To cook food gently in liquid, just below boiling point, usually with an occasional bubble.

Toss – To combine ingredients with a repeated lifting motion.

Whip – To beat rapidly.

Whisk – A kitchen tool made of wire loops that tends to add air as it mixes substances together.

Measurement Abbreviations

Teaspoon……………………………………………..tsp. or t
Tablespoon……………………………………. tbsp. or Tbsp. or T
Cup………………………………………………………….c. or C
Quart………………………………………………………………..qt
Ounce……………………………………………………………….oz
Pint…………………………………………………………………..Pt
Large………………………………………………………………Lrg
Small……………………………………………………………… sm
Gallon…………………………………………………………….gal
Inch…………………………………………………………………in
Pound……………………………………………………………….lb
Fahrenheit……………………………………………………...F
Degree……………………………………………………………..°
Less than…………………………………………………………..<

Conversions

Dash	=	2 or 3 drops (liquid) or less than 1/8 teaspoon (dry)
1 tablespoon	=	3 teaspoons or ½ ounce
2 tablespoons	=	1 ounce
1/4 cup	=	4 tablespoons or 2 ounces
1/3 cup	=	5 tablespoons plus 1 teaspoon
1/2 cup	=	8 tablespoons or 4 ounces
3/4 cup	=	12 tablespoons or 6 ounces
1 cup	=	16 tablespoons or 8 ounces
1 pint	=	2 cups or 16 ounces or 1 pound
1 quart	=	4 cups or 2 pints
1 gallon	=	4 quarts
1 pound	=	16 ounces

Index of Recipes

B

Basic Chinese Hot Sauce for Stir Fry - Ray Halpin, 22

Better than Basic Chili - Ray Halpin, 27

Bobotie (African Dish) - Clinton Miller, Jr., 34

Broken Glass Torte - Francena Brantley, 58

Brownies - Tanari Ridley, 53

Bruschetta - Ray Halpin, 3

Buttermilk Biscuits - Penny Simmons, 12

C

Caramelized Apple Cake - Jo Ann Pringle, 56

Chicken, Shrimp & Andouille Jambalaya - Ray Halpin, 46

Chocolate Peanut Butter Brownies - Guy A. Holley, 55

Coconut Pound Cake - Jackie M. Ridley, 57

Corn Muffins - Topeka Ridley, 11

Corn Pudding - Derek Peters, 77

Cream Cheese Pound Cake - Jacqueline McNeil, 51

D

Daddy's Barbeque Sauce - Clinton Miller, Jr., 24

Dim Sum Dipping Sauce - Ray Halpin, 22

E

Easy Lemon Pound Cake - Mary Green, 49

F

Fresh Basil Pesto - Francena Brantley, 21

Fried Okra - from Jacque's Recipe Box, 77

G

Ground Turkey Skillet Casserole - Barbara Sidney, 45

H

Hoecake Bread - Yovonda R. Jones, 13

Honey Angel Biscuits - Aunt Eliza Miller, 14

Hot and Spicy Collard Greens - Lititiah D. Youman, 78

I

Italian Party Bites - from Jacque's Recipe Box, 5

L

Lemon Cheese Pie - Penny Simmons, 54

M

Marinated Collards and Cabbage Salad - Francena Brantley, 23

Meatballs - Ray Halpin, 6

My BBQ Sauce - Ray Halpin, 22

N

New England Clam Chowder - Bob dell Elba, 26

O

Old Fashioned Apple Crisp - Francena Brantley, 50

Old Fashioned Pound Cake - Francena Brantley, 53

Old-fashioned Lemonade - Drew Miller, 3

Old-fashioned Plain Cake - Jo Ann Pringle, 49

P

Parker House Rolls - Reba Anderson Graham, 15

Party Meatballs - Francena Brantley, 6

Pasta Shells with Smoked Turkey - Nicole Miller, 40

Peach Cobbler - Aunt Eliza Miller, 59

Pecan Glazed Pumpkin Pie - Tonique Moore, 52

Pineapple-Carrot Juice - H. Jerome Youman III, 3

Portuguese Grilled Chicken - Ray Halpin, 40

Potato Salad - Gloria Owens, 21

R

Rack of Lamb - Jeanette S. Miller, 33

Rib Rub - Ray Halpin, 35

Rice and Chicken - from Jacque's Recipe Box, 41

S

San Francisco Chicken – Deconstructed Ray Halpin, 42

San Francisco Chicken Breasts - Ray Halpin, 44

Super-Party Nachos - from Jacque's Recipe Box, 7

Sweet N Sour Meatballs - Mary Green, 5

Sweet Potato Biscuits - Quiyon Peters, 11

Sweet Potato Pound Cake - Francena Brantley, 50

T

Turkey Meatloaf - John B. Sidney, 43

Turkey Sausage Rolls - Earl E. Miller, 7

Turkey Sausage, Peppers and Onions - from Jacque's Recipe Box, 41

W

Wild Turkey Soup - Jairus Howell, 25

Y

Yorkshire Beef - from Jacque's Recipe Box, 32

Index of Contributors

Aunt Eliza Miller 14, 59
Barbara Sidney..45
Bob dell Elba... 26
Clinton Miller, Jr... 24, 34
Derek Peters..77
Drew Miller..3
Earl E. Miller..7
Francena Brantley...............................6, 21, 23, 50, 53, 58
from Jacque's Recipe Box..............................5, 7, 32, 41, 77
Gloria Owens...21
Guy A. Holley.. 55
H. Jerome Youman III..3
Jackie M. Ridley...57
Jacqueline McNeil..51
Jacquelyn Miller..5, 7, 32, 41, 77
Jairus Howell...25
Jeanette S. Miller...33
Jo Ann Pringle...49
John B. Sidney...43
Lititiah D. Youman...78
Mary Green..5, 49
Nicole Miller..40
Penny Simmons...12, 54
Quiyon Peters..11

Ray Halpin.............................3, 6, 22, 27, 35, 40, 42, 44, 46

Reba Anderson Graham...15

Tanari Ridley...53

Tonique Moore...52

Topeka Ridley..11

Yovonda R. Jones 13

Notes